Highlights Hidden Pictures

AMAZING NATURE PUZZLES

HIGHLIGHTS PRESS
Honesdale, Pennsylvania

Welcome, Hidden Pictures Puzzlers!

When you finish a puzzle, check it off ☑. Good luck, and happy puzzling!

Contents

- Butterfly Garden 4–5
- Horsing Around 6
- Forest Friends 7
- I Lava Volcanoes!................. 8
- Prairie Pals 9
- The Great "Art-Doors"........... 10
- Fishing Together 11
- Community Cleanup.......... 12–13
- Flutter By.......................... 14
- Toasty Marshmallows 15
- Birdseed Breakfast............... 16
- Crossing the Creek............... 17
- Tree Talk 18
- Search the Sky................... 19
- The New Kid 20
- Gathering Nuts 21
- Hyena Hilarity.................... 22
- See the Manatees? 23
- Hummingbird's Supper..... 24–25
- Tiny Forest Parade 26
- Snowbound Bison................ 27
- Romping Rhino................... 28
- Fish for Lunch!................... 29
- Drinking Nectar.................. 30
- Fancy Flamingos 31
- Garden Games.................... 32
- Baby Gators....................... 33
- Glamorous Jellyfish.............. 34
- Playful Puffins..................... 35
- Dolphin Day 36–37
- Bugging Out 38
- Aurora Adventure 39
- Meet the Lemurs 40
- That's a Hoot! 41
- Majestic Sequoia 42
- Air Traffic 43
- Ribbits and Moos................ 44
- Olivia's Garden Bugs............. 45
- Life on the Reef.............. 46–47
- So Many Leaves!................. 48
- Going with the Flow 49
- Neck-and-Neck................... 50
- Howling to the Moon 51
- Panda's Party 52–53
- Pond Explorers 54
- Goodnight, Willow 55
- Enjoying *Neigh*-ture 56
- A Bear-y Good Time 57
- *Bzzz*-y Bees...................... 58
- Sunday Bike Ride................. 59
- Reptiles and Amphibians....... 60
- Home, Sweet Home.............. 61
- Pond Pals...................... 62–63
- *Croak* and Croon 64
- Soaring Squirrels 65
- Take a Hike 66

Cover art by Tim Davis

- Enter the Ring!................... 67
- Dragonfly Eyes.............. 68–69
- No Napping 70
- Desert Night 71
- Keepers of the Forest........... 72
- Record Finish 73
- Fresh Catch 74
- Looking for Ants................. 75
- Leaps and Laughs............76–77
- Geyser Surprise................... 78
- Caterpillar Climbers........... 79
- Paddlin' Platypus................ 80
- Ride the Rapids................... 81
- Yard Cleanup..................... 82
- Ring-Tail Tales................... 83
- Busy Beavers..................... 84
- Cute Koalas 85
- On the Galapagos........... 86–87
- Making a Splash 88
- Bear Family X-ing 89
- Lovely Landscape 90
- Whale Watch 91
- Lazy Lizard....................... 92
- Who's There? 93
- Southwestern Sights........ 94–95
- Wild Water Hole.................. 96
- Campsite Critters................. 97
- Where's My Shadow?........... 98
- Duck, Duck, Frog 99
- Snowy Owl Skiers 100–101
- Hiking Hedgehogs 102
- Chilling Out..................... 103
- A Shiver of Sharks.............. 104
- Snowshoe Trail.................. 105
- Follow the Swallows 106
- Summer Clubhouse............. 107
- River Rides 108–109
- I Spy............................. 110
- A Nice Umbrella 111
- Backyard Balance Beam........ 112
- Jitterbug Joy..................... 113
- Mighty Humpback...........114–115
- Desert Deadlock................. 116
- Trying Their Wings 117
- Forest Frolic..................... 118
- Lots to Watch.................... 119
- Rail Bike Trail....................120
- Bird-Watchers.................... 121
- Fleas, If You Please............. 122
- Monkey Meetup 123
- Fishing Buddy 124
- My First S'more 125
- Zoo Crew 126–127
- Majestic Moose 128
- Terrific Toucan 129
- Answers.................... 130–144

Butterfly Garden

snowman

golf tee

artist's brush

saltshaker

popcorn

arrow

seashell

party horn

whale

sock

pointy hat

teacup

butter knife

fishhook

sailboat

4

pennant

ruler

needle

musical note

crown

toy top

snow cone

open book

tooth

heart

slice of pie

nail

magician's wand

slice of pizza

iron

Horsing Around

glove

necktie

ice-cream bar

ladle

banana

candle

boot

wrench

tape dispenser

artist's brush

tweezers

flag

slice of bread

feather duster

turnip

iron

leaf

sailboat

grapes

Art by Chuck Dillon

Forest Friends

musical note

fork

carrot

artist's brush

golf club

crown

baseball cap

shoe

paper airplane

nail

mug

wishbone

ice-cream cone

pencil

mitten

glove

heart

Art by Mike DeSantis

7

I Lava Volcanoes!

muffin

ruler

radish

slice of pizza

teacup

banana

crescent moon

crown

bird

envelope

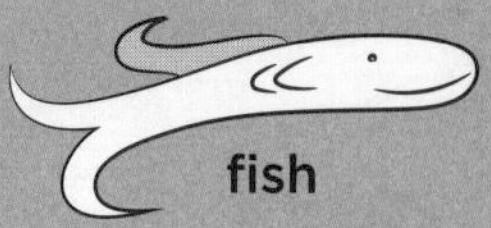

fish

toothbrush

frog

sailboat

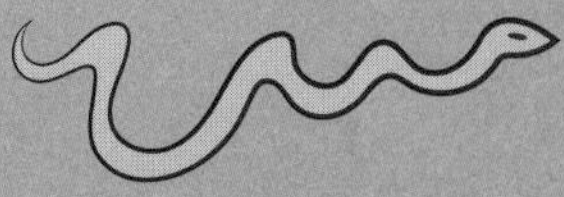

snake

Art by Tamara Petrosino

Prairie Pals

feather

banana

handbell

pennant

safety pin

crescent moon

shoe

bowl

baseball cap

egg

spoon

sailboat

shuttlecock

heart

light bulb

tooth

Art by Rocky Fuller

9

The Great "Art-Doors"

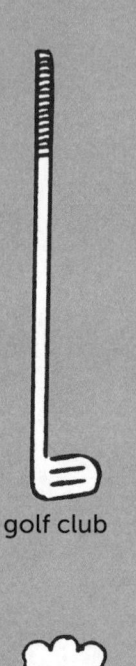

golf club

ice-cream cone

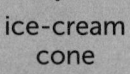

flag

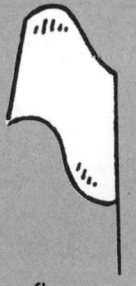

drinking straw

crescent moon

candle

heart

tube of toothpaste

saw

toothbrush

cracker

funnel

glove

wrench

Art by Ron Lieser

10

Fishing Together

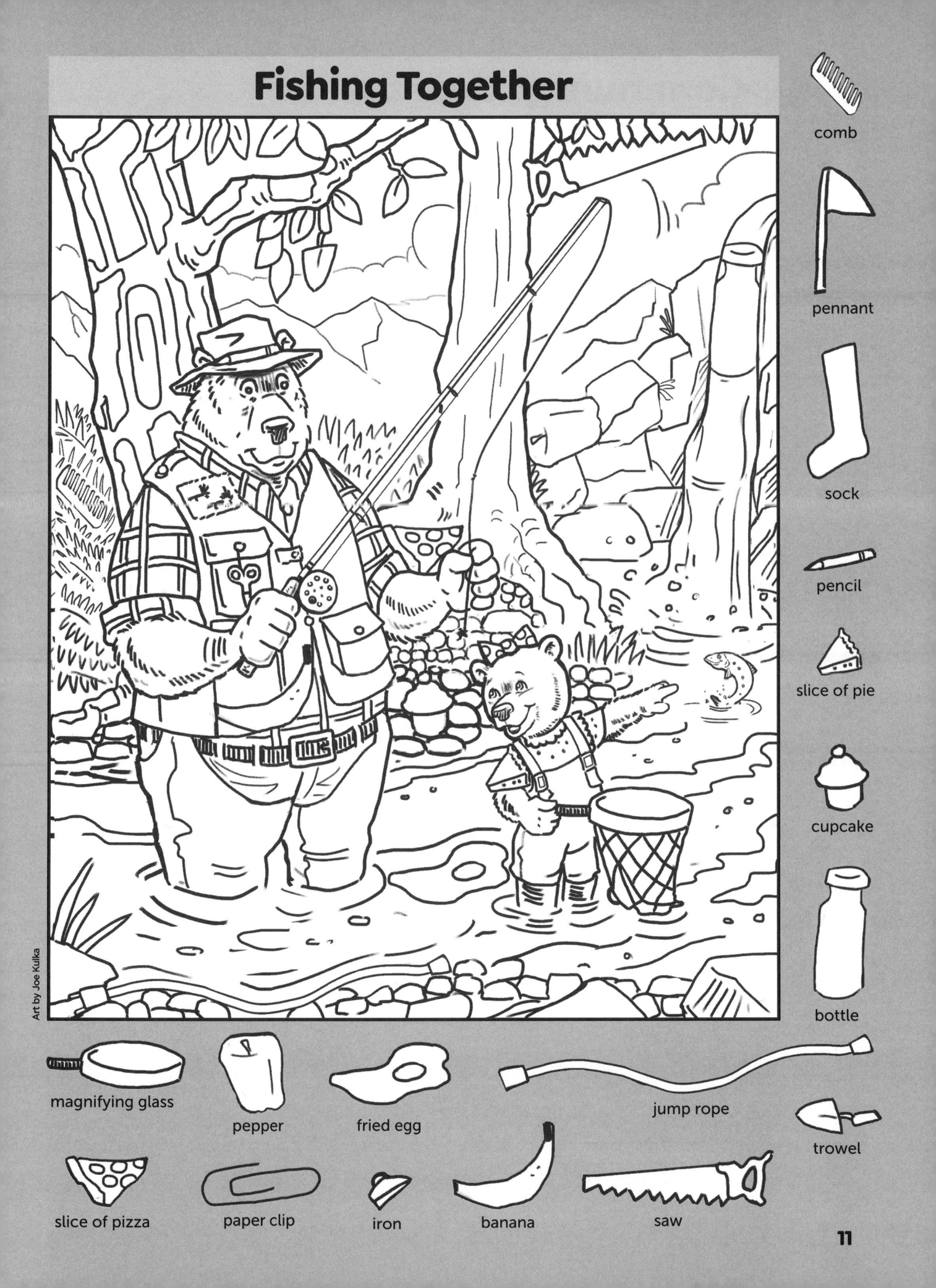

comb

pennant

sock

pencil

slice of pie

cupcake

bottle

magnifying glass

pepper

fried egg

jump rope

trowel

slice of pizza

paper clip

iron

banana

saw

Art by Joe Kulka

Community Cleanup

crescent moon

bell

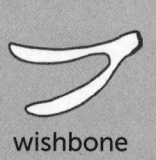

wishbone

wedge of lemon

comb

CITY PARK

ruler

fried egg

slice of pie

horseshoe

crayon

drumstick

envelope

broccoli

drinking
straw

Art by Dana Regan

flag

fish

game piece

pen

toothbrush

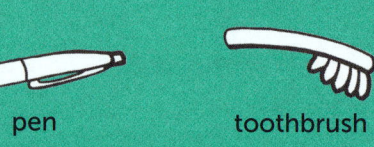

seashell

13

Flutter By

candle

necktie

closed
umbrella

baseball bat

carrot

pen

sock

banana

slice of pizza

hot dog

frying pan

comb

eyeglasses

button

ice-cream
cone

saltshaker

spoon

pencil

artist's brush

ice pop

slipper

Art by Lyn Martin

Toasty Marshmallows

wishbone

lollipop

candle

needle

flyswatter

pennant

light bulb

boomerang

boot

mug

bell

mallet

comb

spoon

banana

15

Birdseed Breakfast

pencil

ice-cream cone

sock

ice-cream bar

mushroom

fish

cupcake

spoon

Crossing the Creek

yo-yo

candy cane

funnel

spoon

jump rope

pencil

wedge of lemon

saltshaker

tooth

hamburger

ice pop

artist's brush

needle

lightning bolt

hairbrush

fish

sailboat

tomato

Art by Laura Close

17

Tree Talk

ladle

spoon

flowerpot

lollipop

propeller hat

butter knife

bowl

string bean

eyeglasses

toothbrush

tooth

shoe

slice of pizza

teacup

whale

Art by Laura Close

18

Search the Sky

Art by Leighanne Schneider

pennant

golf club

ring

mitten

drinking straw

ice-cream cone

slice of pie

toothbrush

feather

paper clip

envelope

comb

spoon

candy cane

fishhook

The New Kid

ice-cream cone

pennant

fork

boot

screw

needle

trowel

mug

candy corn

heart

drinking glass

banana

paper clip

snake

lizard

20

Art by Maggie Swanson

Gathering Nuts

carrot

artist's brush

necktie

feather

ruler

crescent moon

drumstick

snail

caterpillar

pencil

tack

mushroom

slice of pie

ladybug

fish

21

Hyena Hilarity

thimble

pencil

glove

peanut

broccoli

feather duster

lightning bolt

knitted hat

comb

banana

puzzle piece

cleat

potato

closed umbrella

belt

carrot

wristwatch

mitten

Art by Brian Michael Weaver

22

See the Manatees?

carrot

lollipop

scissors

arrow

pennant

magician's wand

needle

jump rope

high-heeled shoe

open book

funnel

kite

sailboat

broccoli

heart

pear

banana

bowl

frying pan

spoon

ruler

Art by Laura Close

Hummingbird's Supper

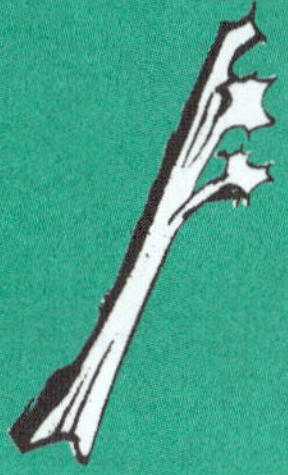

celery

umbrella

fishhook

horn

spoon

needle-nose
pliers

24

pennant

clamshell

pear

heart

paddle

needle

arrow

slipper

Art by Rocky Fuller

25

Tiny Forest Parade

artist's brush

yo-yo

turnip

vase

yam

crescent moon

candle

seashell

carrot

crown

slice of pie

eyeglasses

tomato

mushroom

snake

wishbone

egg

banana

canoe

Art by Gary Mohrman

26

Snowbound Bison

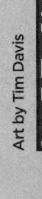
Art by Tim Davis

feather

dog

fish

comb

slice of pie

frog

dolphin

rat

turtle

rabbit

spoon

pencil

saw

bat

27

Romping Rhino

artist's brush

rose

baseball bat

tack

fork

paddle

golf club

slice of cake

football

nail

spoon

rowboat

string bean

slice of pizza

trowel

whale

fish

pie

bowl

pitchfork

party hat

snake

Art by Joe Seidita

28

Fish for Lunch!

banana

heart

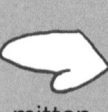
mitten

flag

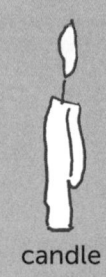
candle

wishbone

Art by Samantha Bell

artist's brush

muffin

crown

comb

sneaker

magnet

slice of pie

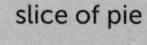
scissors

29

Drinking Nectar

banana

dolphin

crescent moon

cinnamon bun

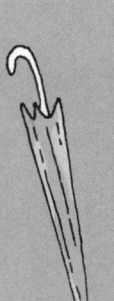
closed umbrella

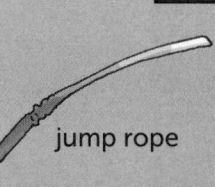
jump rope

Art by Scot Ritchie

yo-yo

balloons

baseball cap

arrowhead

doughnut

seashell

party hat

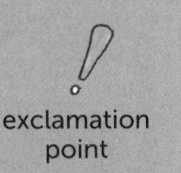
exclamation point

30

Fancy Flamingos

flag

party hat

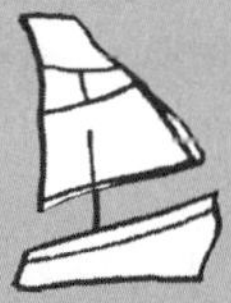

sailboat

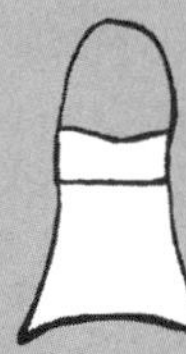

apron

hat

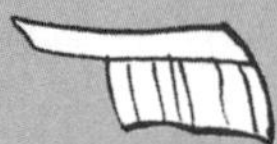

hairbrush

banana

rabbit

mushroom

heart

tack

beet

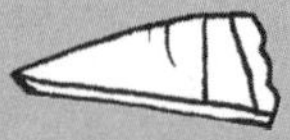

slice of pie

Art by Katy Plemmons

31

Garden Games

wedge of lemon

carrot

ice-cream cone

candy cane

artist's brush

crescent moon

saltshaker

tennis racket

candle

slice of pie

fish

sun

seashell

wheel

ladder

wedge of orange

muffin

slice of pizza

comb

lemon

doughnut

Art by Mernie Gallagher-Cole

32

Baby Gators

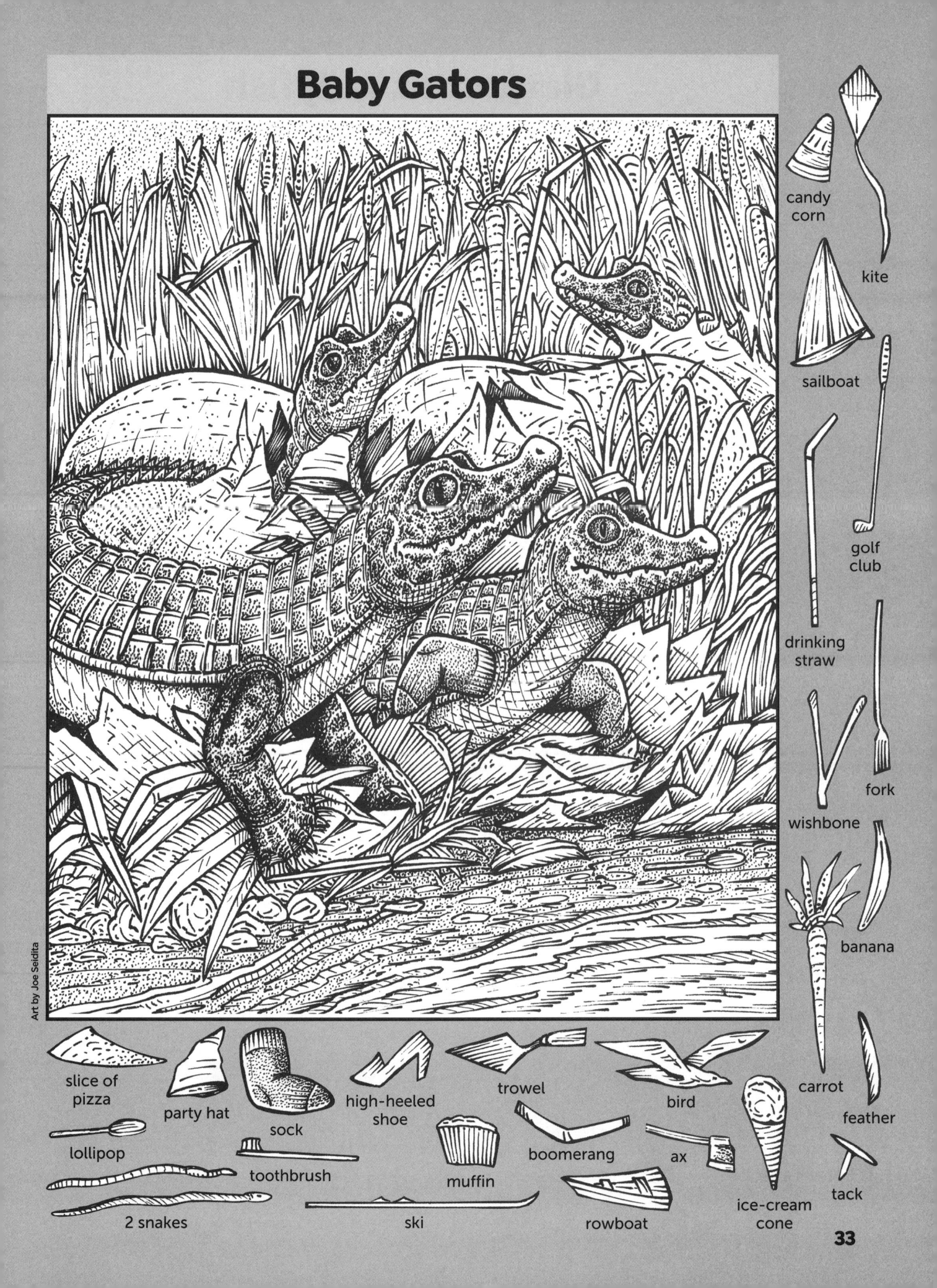

candy corn
kite
sailboat
golf club
drinking straw
fork
wishbone
banana
carrot
feather
tack

slice of pizza
party hat
sock
high-heeled shoe
trowel
bird
lollipop
boomerang
ax
toothbrush
muffin
ice-cream cone
2 snakes
ski
rowboat

Art by Joe Seldita

33

Glamorous Jellyfish

crescent moon

pine tree

candy apple

carrot

wishbone

game piece

muffin

elf's hat

dinosaur

high-heeled shoe

broccoli

hedgehog

eyeglasses

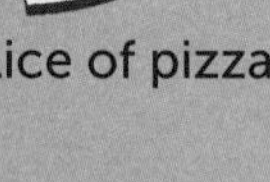

slice of pizza

deer

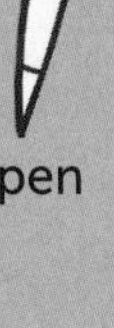

pen

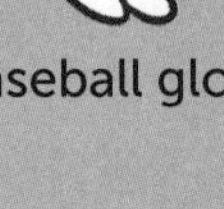

baseball glove

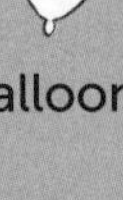

balloon

Art by Chuck Dillon

34

Playful Puffins

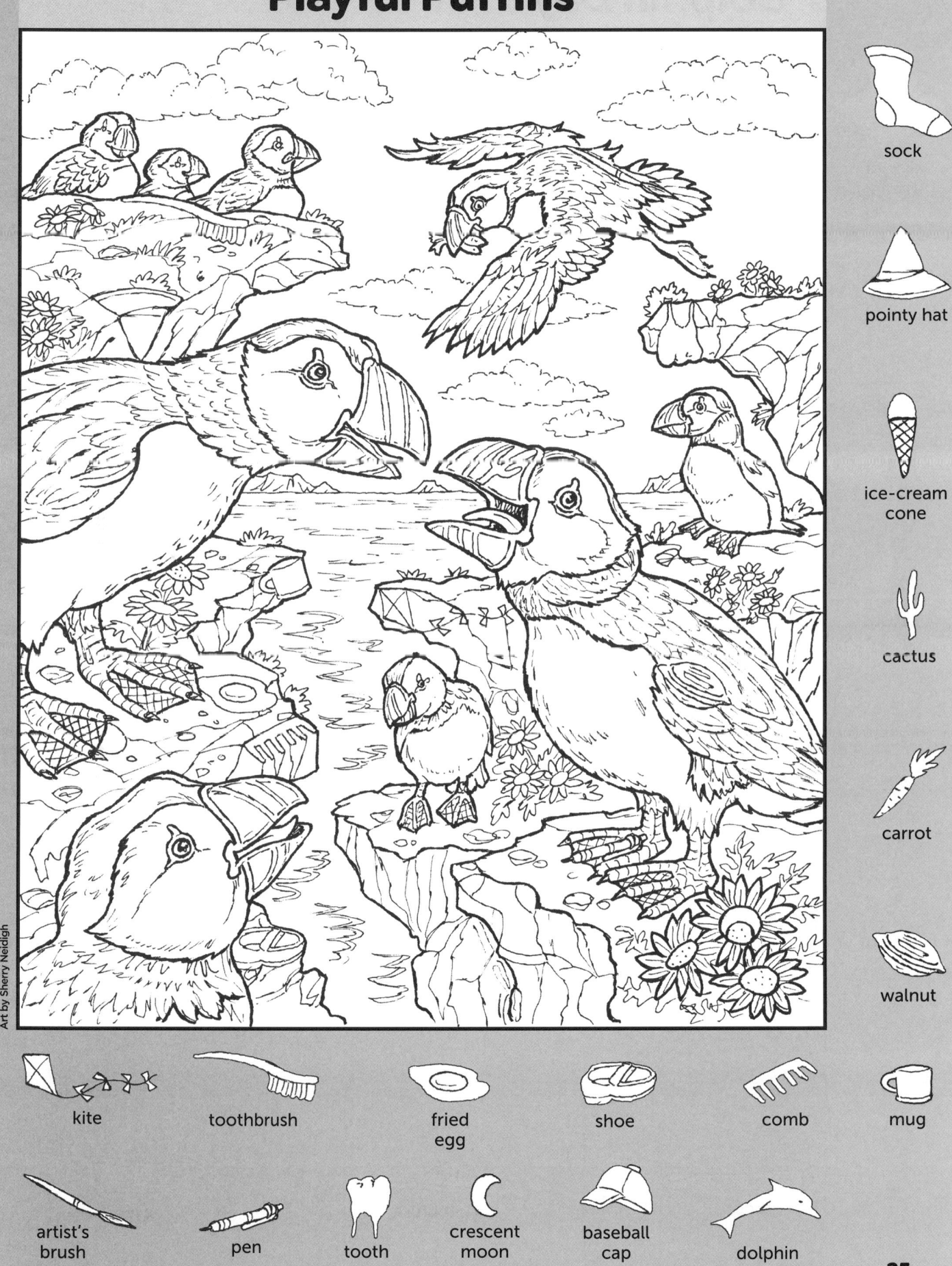

sock

pointy hat

ice-cream cone

cactus

carrot

walnut

kite

toothbrush

fried egg

shoe

comb

mug

artist's brush

pen

tooth

crescent moon

baseball cap

dolphin

35

Dolphin Day

slice of bread

artist's brush

nail

spoon

toothbrush

eyeglasses

36

mitten

peanut

candle

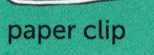

paper clip

feather

sneaker

Art by Karen Stormer Brooks

37

Bugging Out

pen

pencil

golf club

screwdriver

fish

mug

key

slice of cake

ice-cream cone

octopus

shoe

mitten

sailboat

Art by Susan T. Hall

38

Aurora Adventure

cat

leaf

banana

drinking straw

boot

ice-cream bar

fish

fork

bow tie

crown

muffin

arrow

spoon

sock

candle

39

Meet the Lemurs

fork

bowling pin

pushpin

pinecone

star

feather

broom

candle

spoon

candy

comb

ax

key

sneaker

slice of bread

trowel

rabbit

oilcan

fish

teacup

mitten

Art by Sherry Neidigh

40

That's a Hoot!

banana

crayon

necktie

bell

sailboat

golf club

pencil

bean

paper airplane

arrow

football

bucket

fork

ring

flowerpot

sock

ice pop

candy corn

Majestic Sequoia

artist's brush

lightning bolt

pennant

carrot

comb

oar

tweezers

pea pod

hat

fish

paper clip

boomerang

ax

pen

Art by Jon Chad

42

Air Traffic

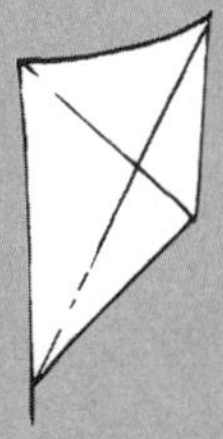

kite

bottle

tent

beehive

glove

musical note

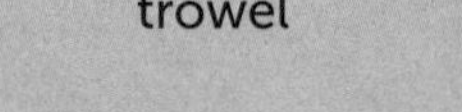

trowel

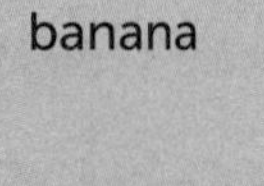

banana

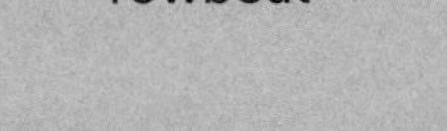

rowboat

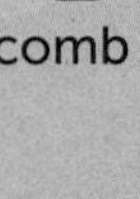

comb

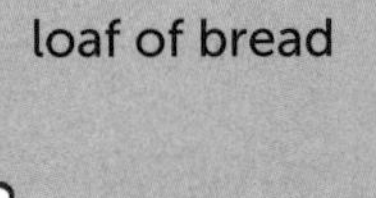

loaf of bread

light bulb

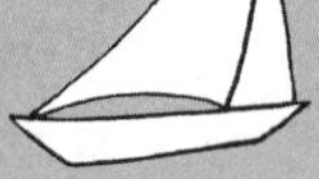

sailboat

teacup

teapot

Art by Kathy Swain-O'Brien

43

Ribbits and Moos

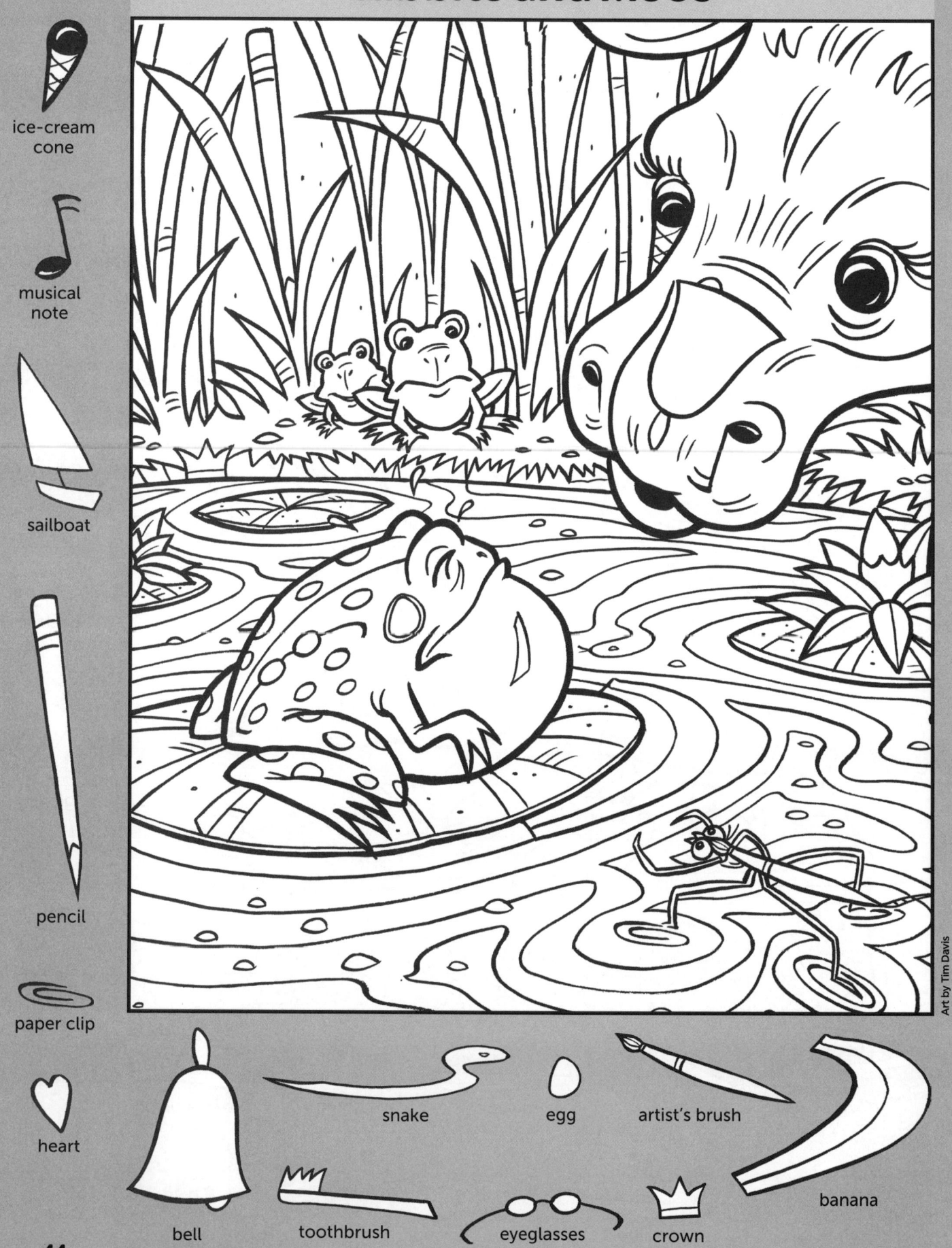

ice-cream cone

musical note

sailboat

pencil

paper clip

heart

bell

toothbrush

snake

egg

eyeglasses

artist's brush

crown

banana

Art by Tim Davis

44

Olivia's Garden Bugs

balloon

baseball bat

scissors

lollipop

cupcake

bell

banana

artist's brush

paper clip

crown

football

rowboat

teacup

sun

gumdrop

slice of cake

slice of watermelon

fish

hot dog

hamburger

sock

Art by Mernie Gallagher-Cole

45

Life on the Reef

baseball bat

key

pine tree

cowboy hat

heart

open book

butterfly

bat

saw

paintbrush

artist's brush

mushroom

bird

46

clothespin

ice-cream cone

carrot

bottle

sock

flower

mug

banana

baseball glove

toothbrush

slice of pie

rabbit

mitten

coffeepot

Art by Maggie Swanson

47

So Many Leaves!

heart

pencil

crayon

baseball bat

fan

kite

comb

ice-cream cone

light bulb

toothbrush

sailboat

domino

crown

teacup

doughnut

diamond

open book

puzzle piece

baseball glove

wedge of lemon

sheep

pineapple

Art by Jennifer Harney

48

Going with the Flow

toy top

lightning bolt

tork

knitted hat

lollipop

needle

broom

ice-cream bar

slice of pizza

spoon

ax

necktie

broccoli

pencil

anchor

comb

magnet

ruler

paper clip

Art by Brian Michael Weaver

49

Neck-and-Neck

crescent moon

banana

needle

broom

ladder

artist's brush

eyeglasses

lollipop

paintbrush

bowl

ring

egg

slice of pizza

Art by Chuck Galey

50

Howling to the Moon

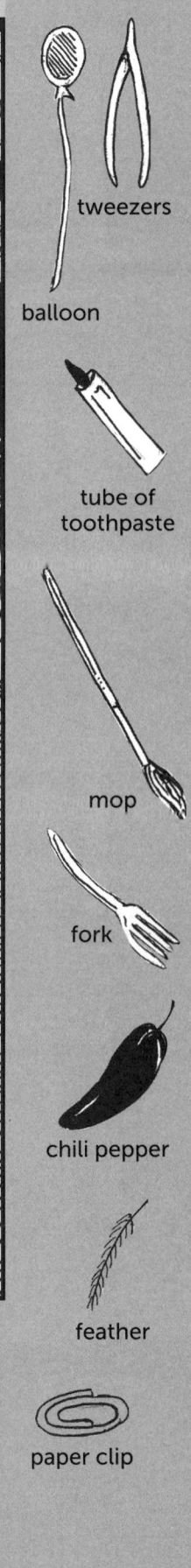

tweezers

balloon

tube of toothpaste

mop

fork

chili pepper

feather

paper clip

moth

boomerang

toothbrush

fried egg

heart

needle

drumstick

comb

popcorn

seal

Art by Rene Mitchell-Mills

51

Panda's Party

dog bone

flashlight

ruler

candle

four-leaf clover

slice of pizza

toothbrush

carrot

banana

fried egg

strawberry

glove

52

crayon

crescent moon

celery

cane

baby's bottle

comb

slice of watermelon

envelope

book

spool of thread

canoe

feather

paw print

Art by Mernie Gallagher-Cole

53

Pond Explorers

crescent moon

banana

sock

ice-cream cone

crown

mug

flowerpot

balloon

horn

hairbrush

light bulb

pencil

snake

apple

heart

bell

ring

lightning bolt

butterfly

54

Art by Laura Close

Goodnight, Willow

pine tree

mushroom

diamond

bell

banana

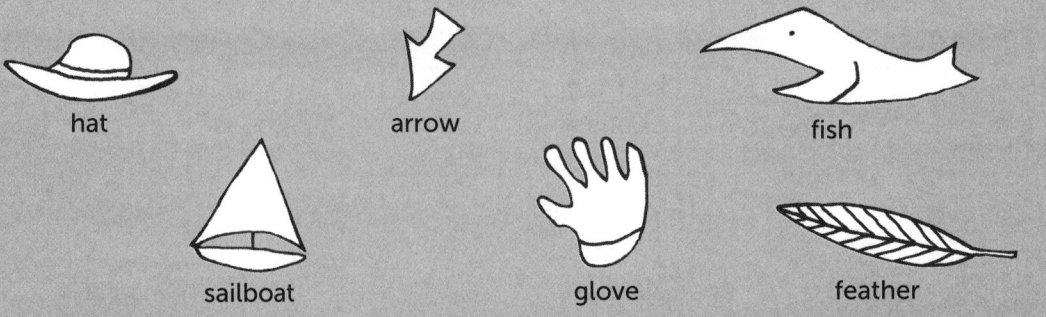

hat

arrow

fish

sailboat

glove

feather

Art by Sonya Montenegro

55

Enjoying *Neigh*-ture

crescent moon

squirrel

fishing pole

needle

pennant

bowl

spatula

toothbrush

bird

rabbit

saltshaker

mouse

frying pan

56

Art by Carolyn Conahan

A Bear-y Good Time

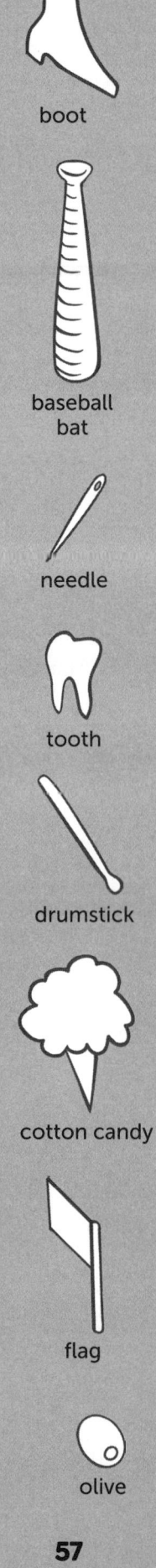

boot

baseball bat

needle

tooth

drumstick

cotton candy

canoe

slice of watermelon

nail

envelope

dog bone

top hat

flag

candy

paper clip

cookie

ruler

broccoli

muffin

banana

fried egg

olive

Art by Bill Golliher

57

Bzzz-y Bees

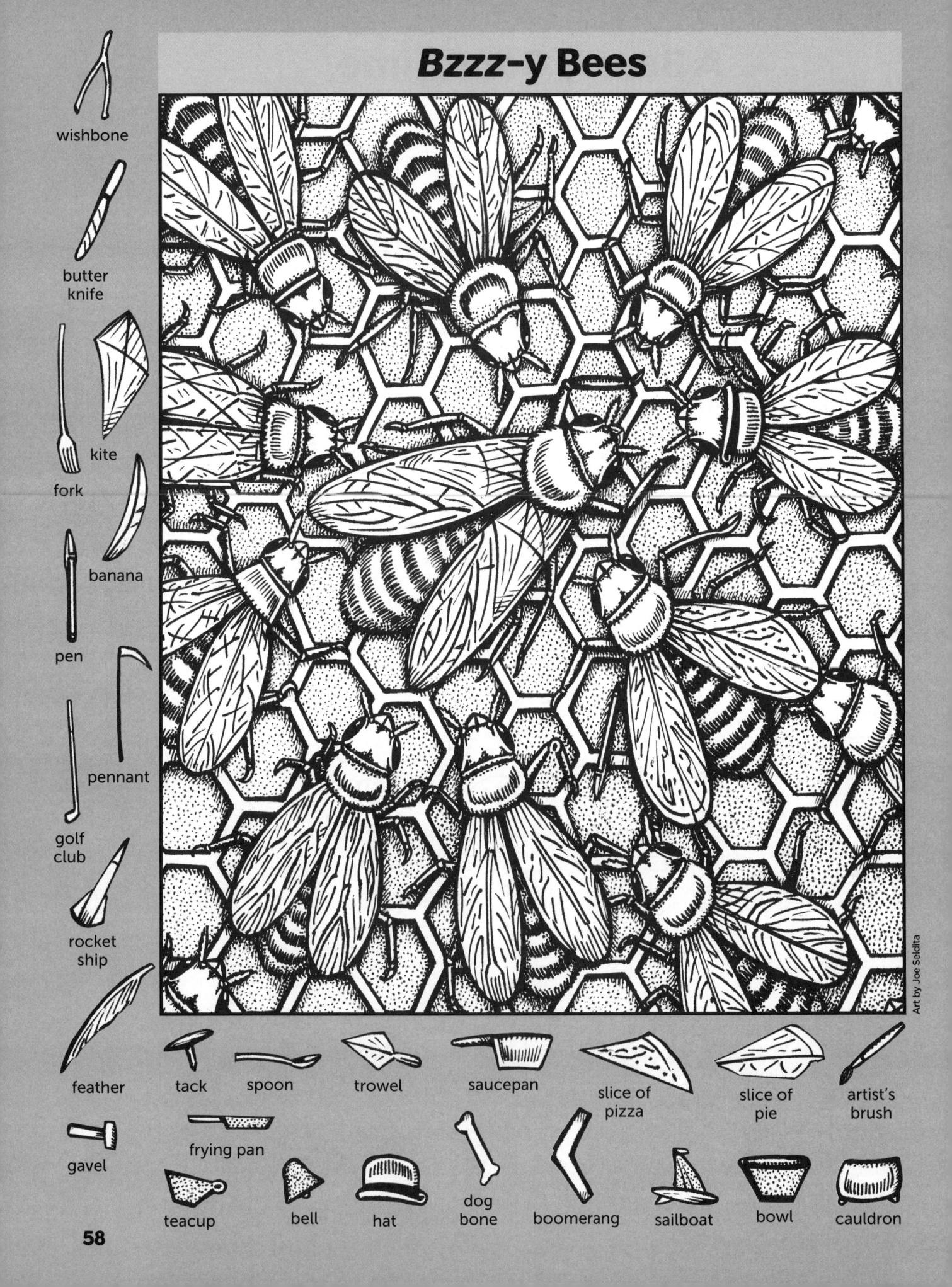

wishbone

butter knife

kite

fork

banana

pen

pennant

golf club

rocket ship

feather

gavel

tack

spoon

trowel

saucepan

slice of pizza

slice of pie

artist's brush

frying pan

teacup

bell

hat

dog bone

boomerang

sailboat

bowl

cauldron

Art by Joe Saldita

Sunday Bike Ride

kite

candle

sock

ice-cream cone

apple
cane

lollipop

seashell

baseball bat

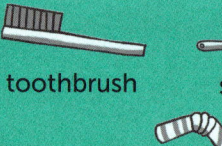
toothbrush

spoon

carrot

spring

pencil

fish

glove

slice of pizza

coat hanger

drinking straw

wedge of lemon

banana

doughnut

heart

Art by Paula Bossio

59

Reptiles and Amphibians

gingerbread cookie

heart

pear

crescent moon

ice-cream cone

seashell

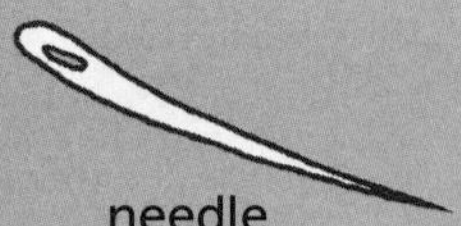

needle

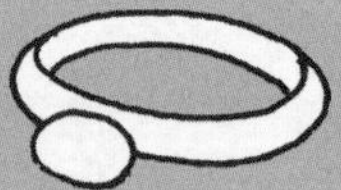

ring

slice of pie

mushroom

crown

fried egg

mouse

peanut

carrot

Art by Sherry Neidgh

60

Home, Sweet Home

mug

saltshaker

eyeglasses

comb

golf club

toothbrush

baseball bat

arrow

kite

ruler

pencil

stamp

button

61

Pond Pals

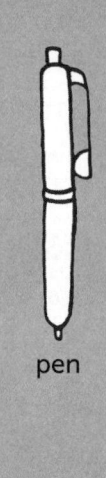

pen

artist's brush

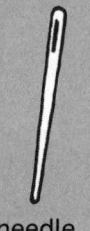

needle

strawberry

closed umbrella

fork

boot

glove

book

spatula

shoe

62

banana

ice-cream cone

handbell

arrow

baseball bat

paper clip

slice of bread

pencil

bottle

wishbone

adhesive bandage

sailboat

teacup

Art by Maggie Swanson

63

Croak and Croon

artist's brush

needle

boot

ice-cream bar

spoon

hoe

fishing net

toothbrush

thimble

teacup

bell

heart

Art by Viki Woodworth

Soaring Squirrels

paper clip

banana

tweezers

ring

glove

cowboy hat

feather

seal

teacup

heart

high-heeled shoe

chicken

spoon

Art by Tim Davis

Take a Hike

hammer

artist's brush

wishbone

drinking straw

candle

pencil

comb

bowl

glove

crown

cupcake

button

swim fin

Art by Ron Lieser

66

Enter the Ring!

paper clip

crescent moon

stethoscope

banana

sailboat

tack

crown

bell

cookie

carrot

comb

rolling pin

ring

light bulb

pencil

67

Dragonfly Eyes

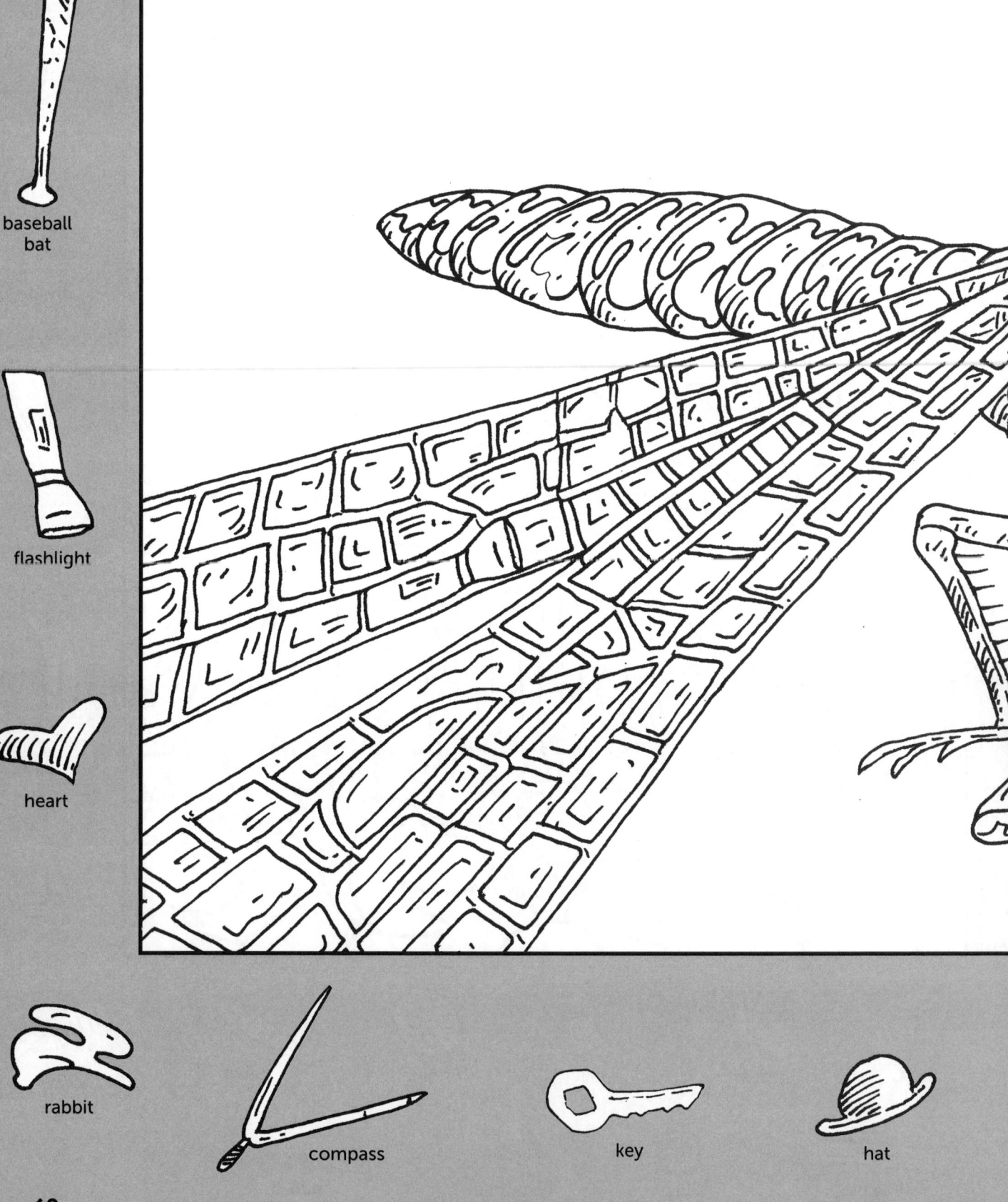

baseball bat

flashlight

heart

rabbit

compass

key

hat

68

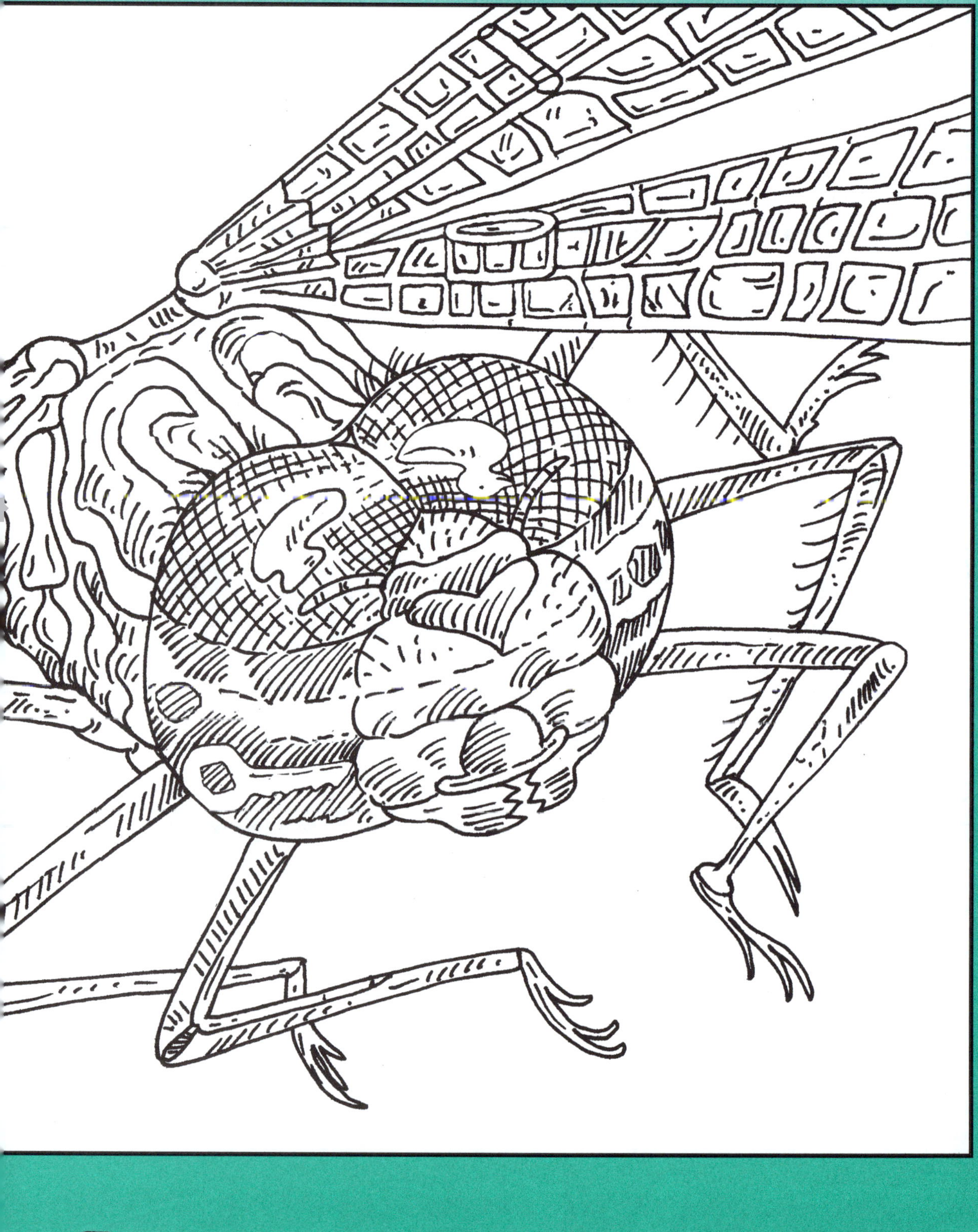

ladder

candle

duck

Art by David Sheldon

mushroom

shuttlecock

drum

69

No Napping

pennant

funnel

needle

banana

carrot

candle

pants

artist's
brush

magnifying
glass

mitten

teacup

ring

toothbrush

heart

chicken

nail

spool
of thread

seashell

crescent
moon

screwdriver

Art by Karen Stormer Brooks

70

Desert Night

pear

drumstick

pitchfork

crescent moon

table-tennis paddle

feather

light bulb

artist's brush

toothbrush

tack

birdhouse

doughnut

candy

envelope

lemon

chili pepper

lightning bolt

Art by Katie Wood

Keepers of the Forest

paper clip

comb

fishhook

pitchfork

rabbit

heart

glove

slice of bread

cat

fish

shoe

snake

spoon

Art by Tim Davis

Record Finish

candle

ruler

party hat

test tube

needle

cane

ice-cream cone

sailboat

butter knife

chili pepper

artist's brush

slice of pie

plate

bell

heart

ring

glove

Art by Gary Mohrman

73

Fresh Catch

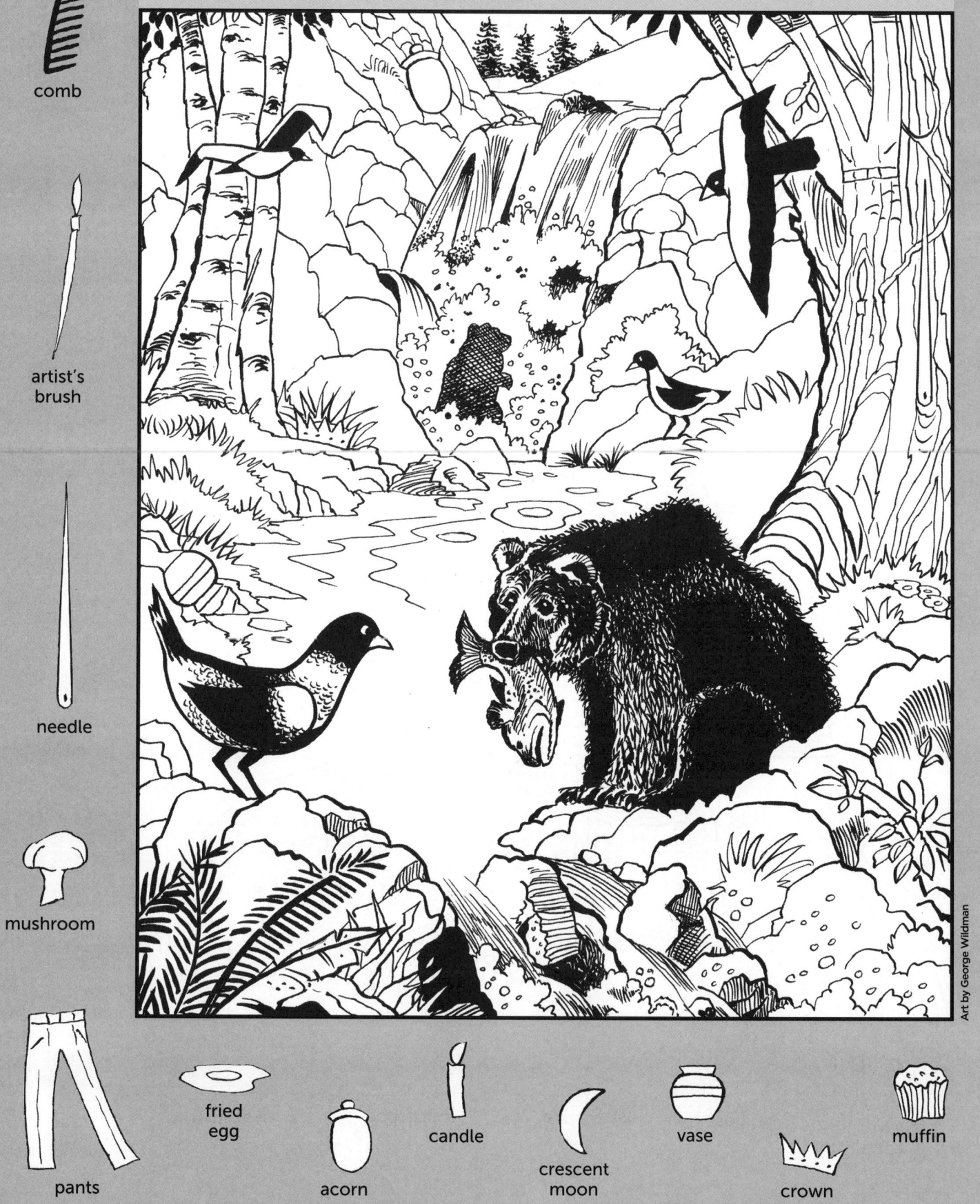

comb

artist's brush

needle

mushroom

pants

fried egg

acorn

candle

crescent moon

vase

crown

muffin

Art by George Wildman

Looking for Ants

scissors

banana

light bulb

handbell

carrot

sock

gingerbread cookie

sheep

shoe

artist's brush

candle

ladle

slice of bread

slice of pizza

wishbone

Art by Maggie Swanson

75

Leaps and Laughs

domino

pennant

carrot

fish

handbell

pitcher

saw

ladder

banana

pencil

knitted hat

paintbrush

slice of pie

envelope

scissors

76

needle

mitten

strawberry

ice-cream cone

artist's brush

key

ruler

toothbrush

mug

heart

gingerbread cookie

elephant

apple

spool of thread

crescent moon

Art by Maggie Swanson

77

Geyser Surprise

needle

pencil

trowel

pear

candle

horseshoe

rabbit

heart

star

whistle

hat

duck

slice of pizza

crescent moon

skateboard

Art by David Sheldon

78

Caterpillar Climbers

sock

crescent moon

pencil

vase

carrot

fishhook

bird

tack

open book

pointy hat

feather

teacup

slice of pie

muffin

boot

79

Paddlin' Platypus

clothespin

crescent moon

beet

artist's palette

boot

dog bone

paper airplane

fried egg

caterpillar

shoe

bowl

comb

Art by George Wildman

80

Ride the Rapids

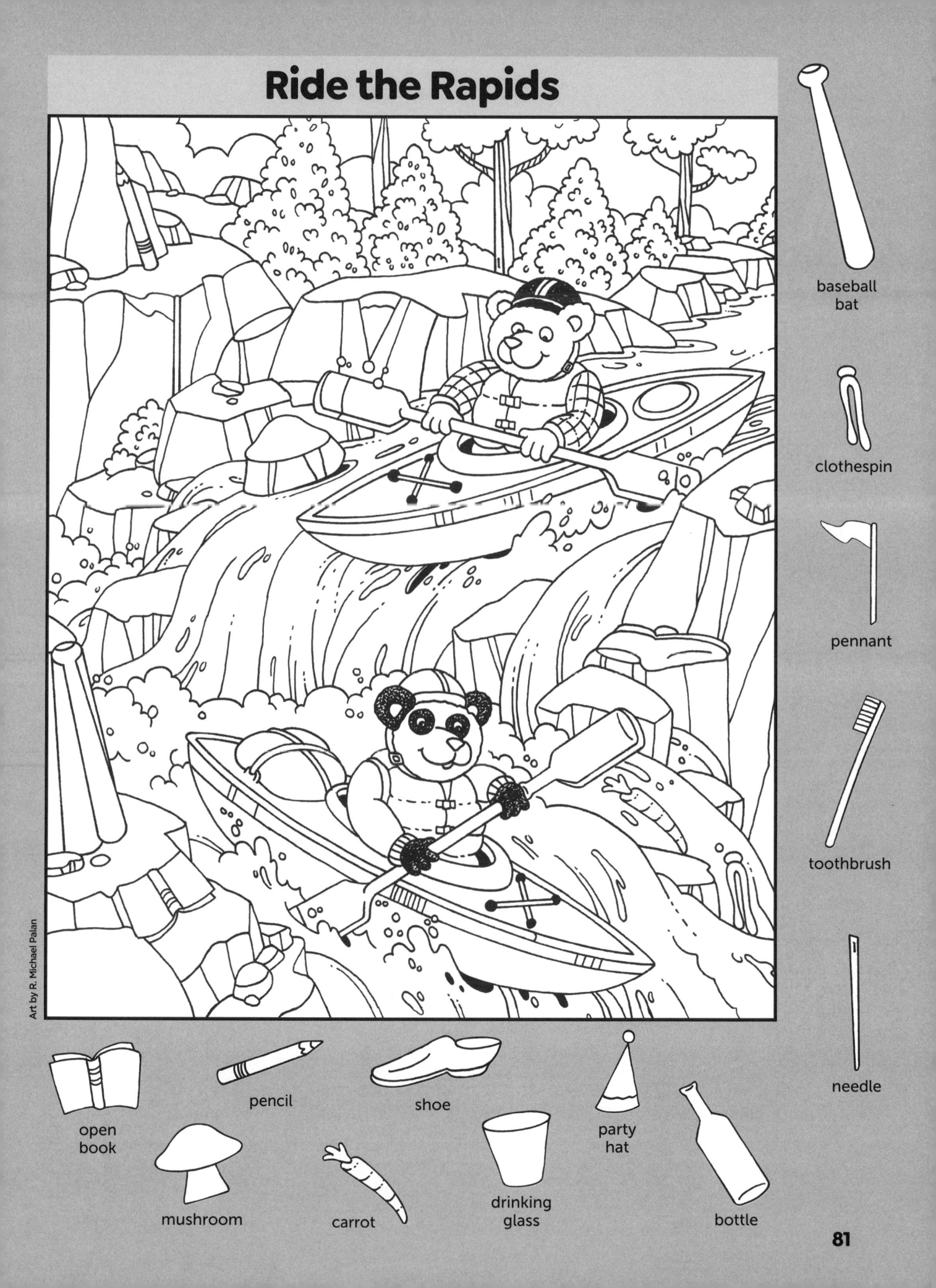

baseball bat

clothespin

pennant

toothbrush

needle

open book

pencil

shoe

party hat

bottle

mushroom

carrot

drinking glass

Art by R. Michael Palan

81

Yard Cleanup

scrub brush

oilcan

pencil

slice of cake

funnel

Art by Ron Lieser

artist's brush

feather

banana

muffin

snake

comb

slice of pie

candle

82

Ring-Tail Tales

WILD TALES FOR RING-TAILS

Art by Kelly Kennedy

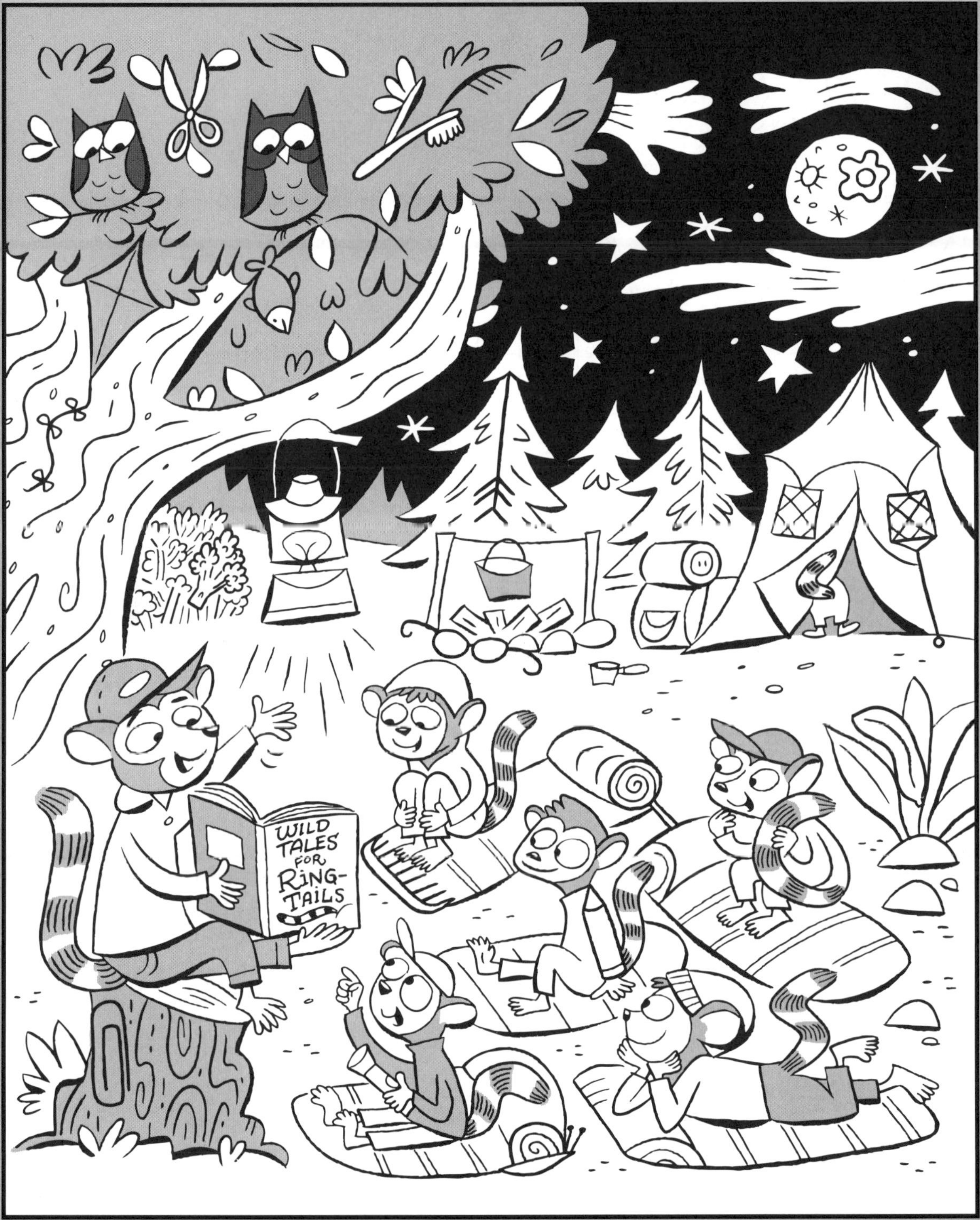

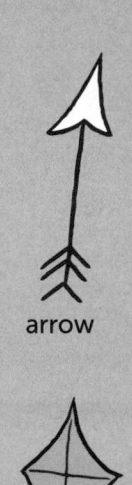

arrow
kite
banana
paper clip
scissors
flyswatter

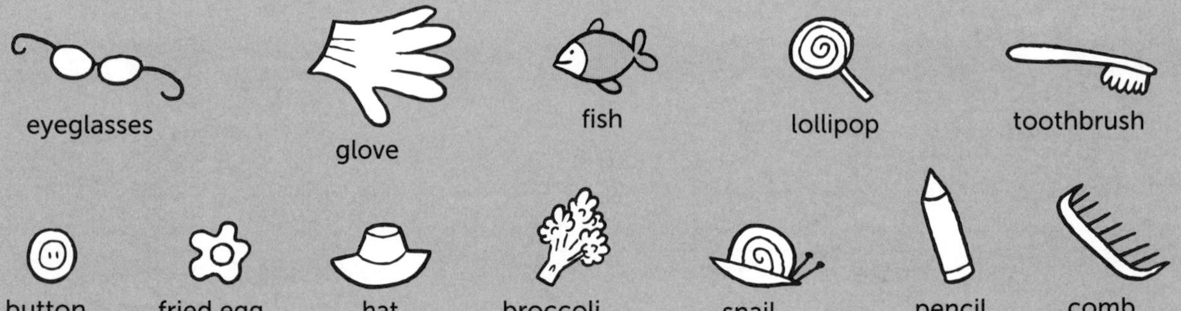

eyeglasses
glove
fish
lollipop
toothbrush
button
fried egg
hat
broccoli
snail
pencil
comb

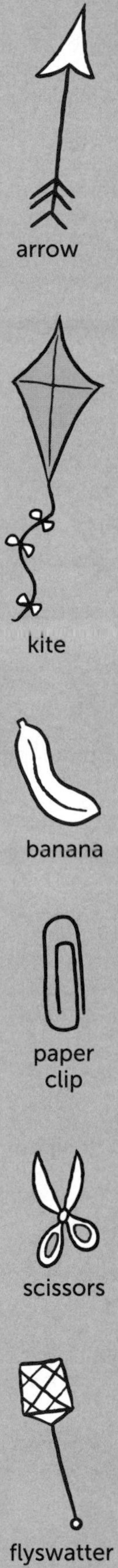

Busy Beavers

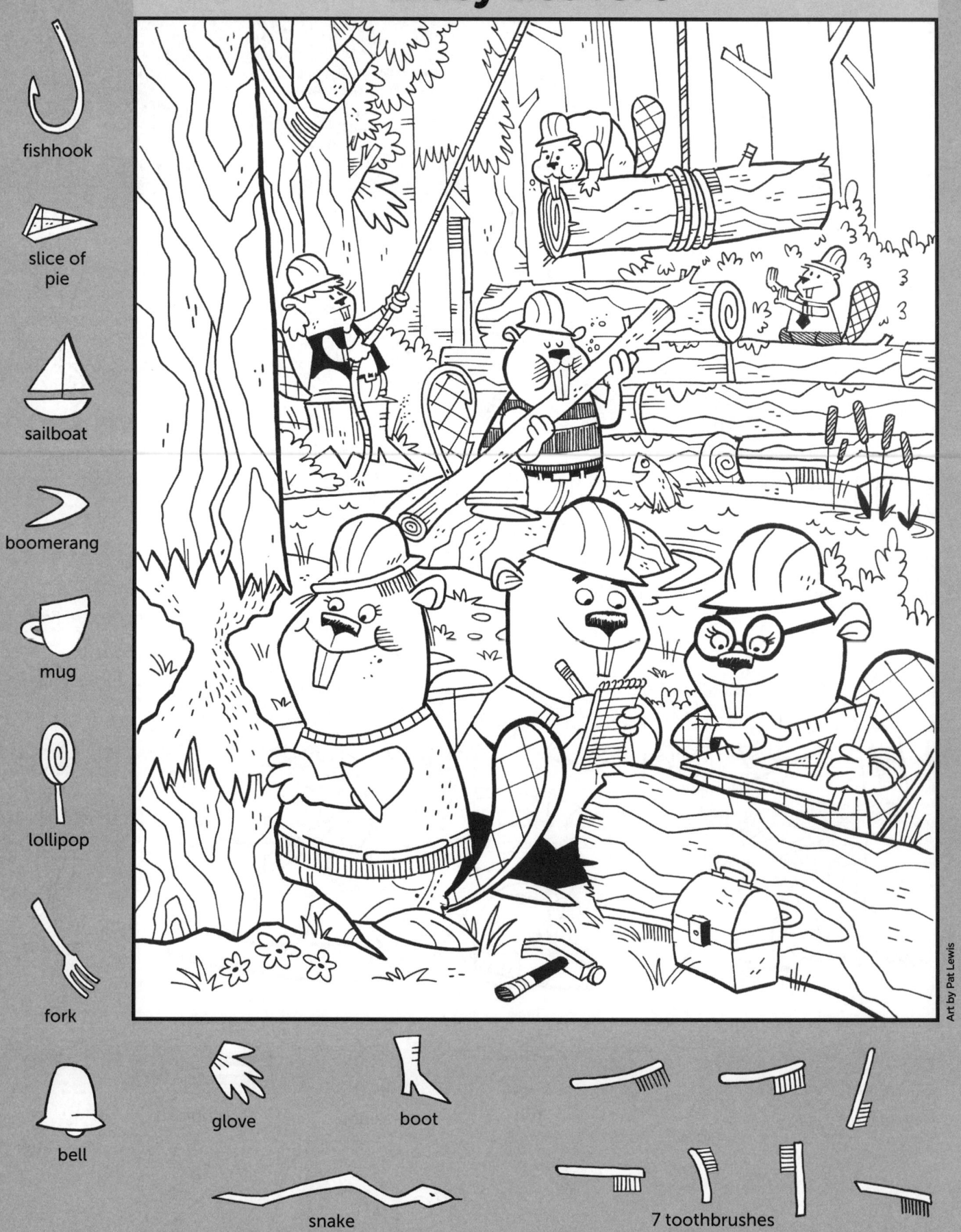

fishhook

slice of pie

sailboat

boomerang

mug

lollipop

fork

bell

glove

boot

snake

7 toothbrushes

Art by Pat Lewis

84

Cute Koalas

candle

artist's brush

hockey stick

mushroom

archer's bow

firefighter's helmet

binoculars

top hat

slice of cake

iron

musical note

bathtub

cowboy hat

prism

sailboat

elf's hat

Art by Mark Corcoran

85

On the Galapagos

mitten

banana

bell

ice-cream cone

artist's brush

spool of thread

open book

pear

cat

dog bone

pencil

86

slice of bread

wishbone

sock

teacup

crescent moon

light bulb

Art by Maggie Swanson

toothbrush

baseball cap

saw

comb

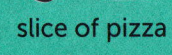

tube of toothpaste

slice of pizza

key

frying pan

87

Making a Splash

heart

pencil

hockey stick

golf club

needle

artist's brush

musical note

balloon

fishhook

shoe

snake

ruler

drinking straw

slice of pizza

sock

boomerang

bell

domino

bowl

ladder

wedge of lemon

glove

crown

sailboat

banana

pennant

Art by Gary LaCoste

Bear Family X-ing

hockey stick

pants

lightning bolt

baseball

party hat

matchstick

sock

boomerang

snail

sailboat

pennant

potato

ring

traffic cone

fish

envelope

toothbrush

shuttlecock

mitten

canoe

Art by Scot Ritchie

89

Lovely Landscape

golf club

needle

nail

wishbone

apple

olive

heart

dolphin

megaphone

safety pin

cowboy hat

slice of pizza

seashell

fried egg

rabbit

rowboat

banana

mug

beetle

strawberry

90

Art by Sherry Neidigh

Whale Watch

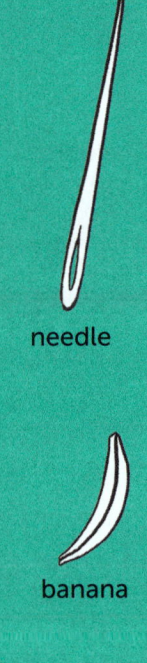
needle

banana

sneaker

musical note

comb

heart

Art by Tim Davis

megaphone

snake

pliers

bird

pencil

toothbrush

spoon

bowling pin

91

Lazy Lizard

broom

kite

ice-cream cone

needle

ruler

star

pennant

ladder

pencil

mug

fish

frying pan

heart

pear

slice of pizza

banana

Art by Paula Bossio

Who's There?

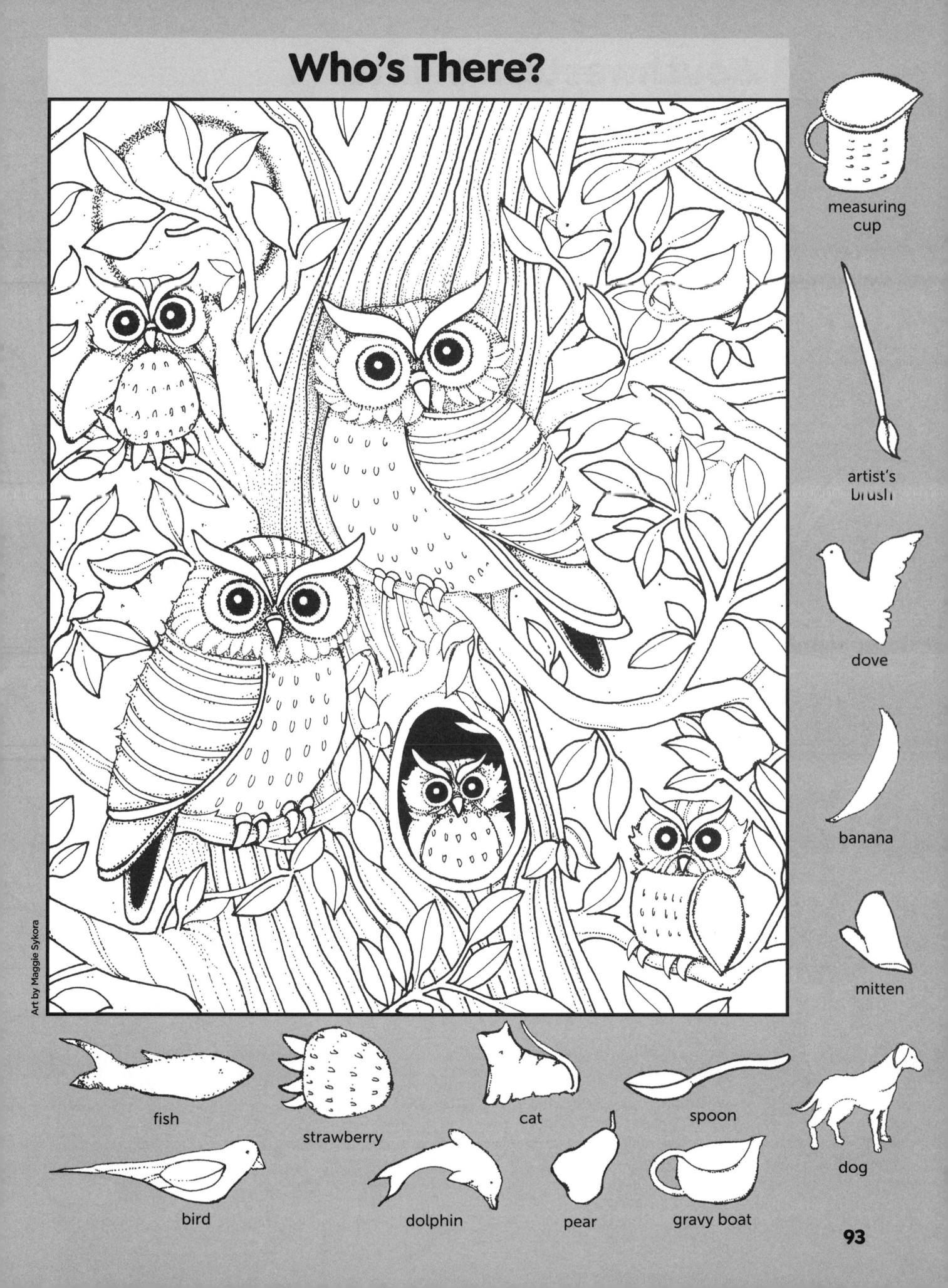

measuring cup

artist's brush

dove

banana

mitten

fish

strawberry

cat

spoon

dog

bird

dolphin

pear

gravy boat

Art by Maggie Sykora

93

Southwestern Sights

matchstick

green bean

lightning bolt

mitten

candle

golf club

wishbone

snowflake

tooth

teacup

heart

popcorn

pickle

adhesive bandage

slice of pizza

dog bone

pig

frying pan

94

fishing
pole

closed
umbrella

needle

Art by Laura Close

saltshaker   flowerpot   crown   balloon   toothbrush

wedge
of lemon   fried
egg   pineapple   crescent
moon   high-heeled
shoe   rolling pin

95

Wild Water Hole

pear

teacup

fishhook

snowman

paper clip

ice-cream cone

lollipop

candy cane

fan

crescent moon

drumstick

cowboy hat

carrot

heart

whale

crown

wedge of lemon

slice of pizza

doughnut

toothbrush

comb

Art by Mernie Gallagher-Cole

96

Campsite Critters

raindrop

feather

fishhook

necktie

candle

ladle

baseball

rake

belt

heart

baseball cap

fish

adhesive bandage

shuttlecock

swim fin

party hat

Art by Scot Ritchie

97

Where's My Shadow?

candle

balloon

pencil

cane

nail

pear

pennant

leaf

fishhook

envelope

heart

comb

spool of thread

musical note

needle

funnel

Art by Sally Springer

98

Duck, Duck, Frog

rocket ship

flag

candle

baseball bat

spatula

mitten

wishbone

nail

mug

heart

needle

artist's brush

banana

crescent moon

comb

Snowy Owl Skiers

spatula

dinosaur

gingerbread cookie

cactus

heart

matchstick

jump rope

fork

wishbone

jellyfish

shoe

star

100

ladle

ice-cream bar

candle

bell

mushroom

sailboat

crown

butterfly

tent

comb

fish

elephant

envelope

Art by Laura Close

101

Hiking Hedgehogs

candle

ice-cream cone

wishbone

scissors

pencil

wedge of lemon

heart

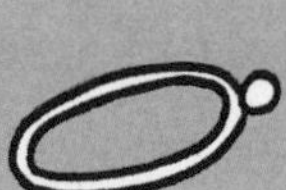

ring

fan

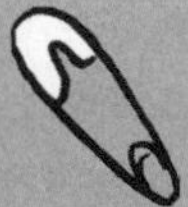

safety pin

baby's rattle

slice of pie

toothbrush

cherry

Art by Leighanne Schneider

102

Chilling Out

sock

spool of thread

pencil

handbell

pennant

candle

sailboat

measuring cup

shoe

fish

crown

spoon

baseball cap

ice-cream cone

rabbit

clothespin

banana

Art by Maggie Swanson

103

A Shiver of Sharks

baseball bat

golf club

sneaker

sailboat

bell

paper clip

needle

heart

tweezers

penguin

slice of pie

toothbrush

104

Snowshoe Trail

closed umbrella

candle

saltshaker

ice-cream cone

rabbit

duck

sailboat

snail

dolphin

fish

mushroom

rowboat

bird

toothbrush

loaf of bread

clothespin

teacup

cowbell

spoon

Art by Linda Weller

105

Follow the Swallows

closed umbrella

boot

mouse

candle

tweezers

shuttlecock

bell

saw

toothbrush

ice-cream cone

heart

fish

glove

carrot

slice of pie

spoon

Art by Tim Davis

106

Summer Clubhouse

necktie

hockey stick

baseball bat

needle

fork

eggplant

game piece

basketball

olive

flute

slice of pie

envelope

rabbit

belt

comb

grapes

wishbone

sheep

beet

boomerang

die

open book

sailboat

Art by Gideon Kendall

107

River Rides

ghost

pennant

whale

slice of pizza

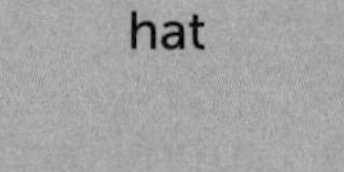

hat

glove

108

drumsticks

cane

coat hanger

plate

frying pan

jump rope

109

I Spy

feather

pencil

ice-cream cone

sock

parrot

glove

sailboat

bow tie

crown

flag

armadillo

wedge of cheese

apple

iron

whale

mushroom

snake

Art by Marlee Harrald-Pilz

110

A Nice Umbrella

cane

heart

pennant

lollipop

sailboat

ring

sock

magnet

toothbrush

hammer

telescope

funnel

mug

needle

spoon

artist's brush

crescent moon

comb

slice of pie

Art by Rocky Fuller

Backyard Balance Beam

handbell

candle

butterfly

carrot

ice-cream
cone

bowling
pin

closed
umbrella

giraffe

scissors

crown

chicken

cupcake

elf's hat

pickax

hat

duck

slice of pie

rowboat

sailboat

fish

Art by Linda Weller

112

Jitterbug Joy

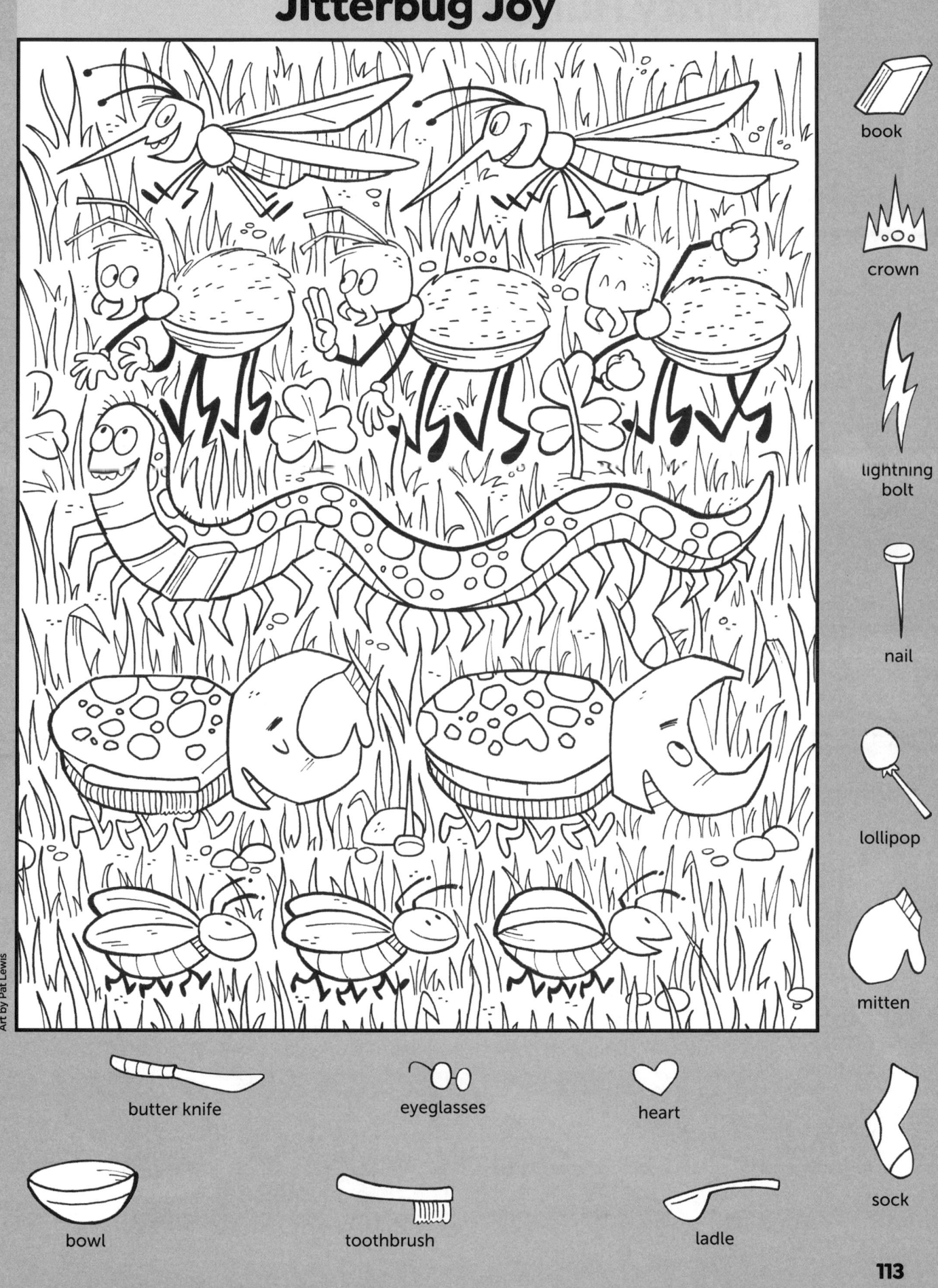

book

crown

lightning bolt

nail

lollipop

mitten

sock

butter knife

eyeglasses

heart

bowl

toothbrush

ladle

113

Mighty Humpback

hoe

ghost

crescent moon

saw

safety pin

snake

114

crayon

bouquet of flowers

banana

slice of pie

pear

envelope

115

Desert Deadlock

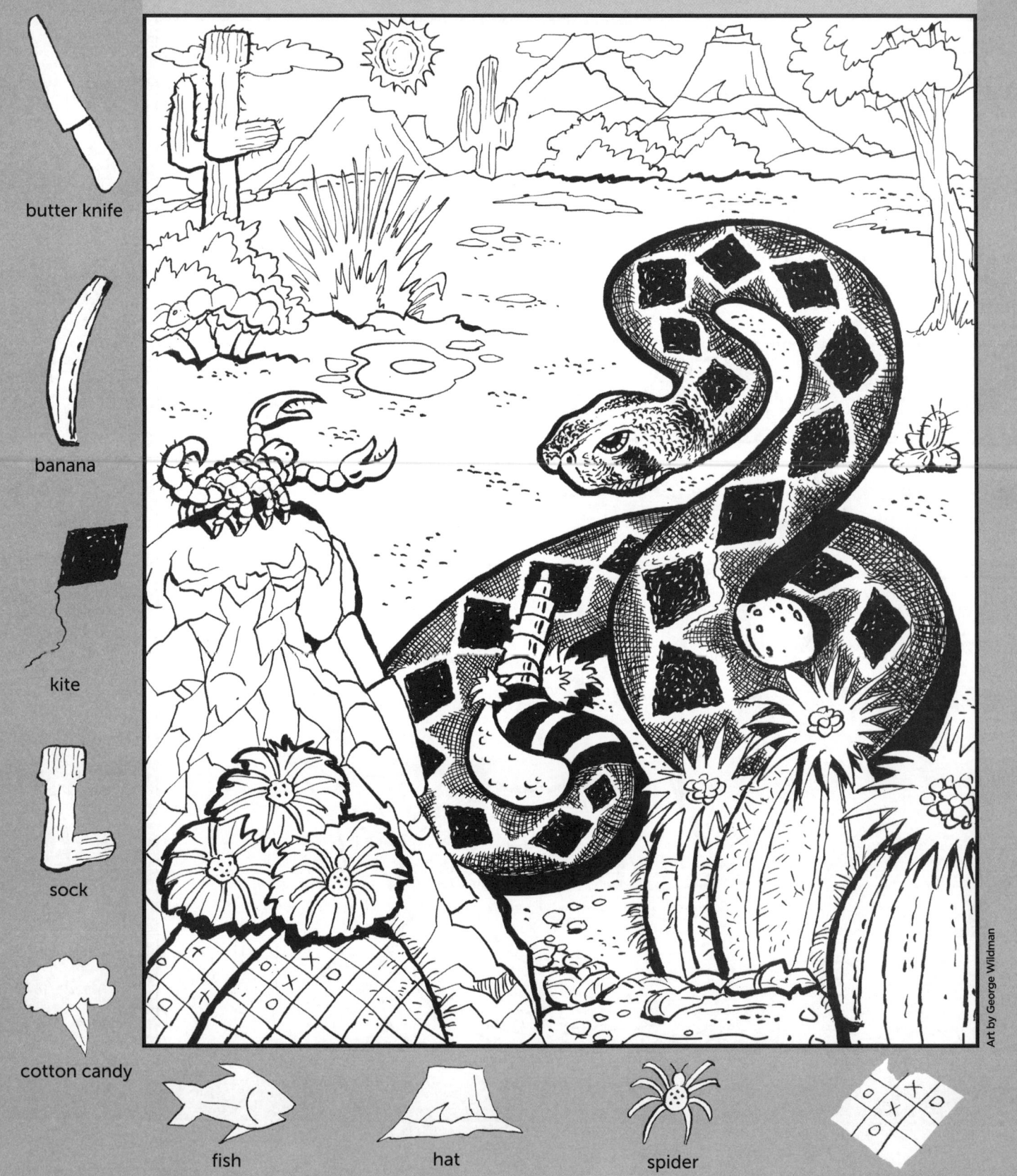

butter knife

banana

kite

sock

cotton candy

fish

hat

spider

tic-tac-toe game

caterpillar

fried egg

lemon

Art by George Wildman

116

Trying Their Wings

sailboat

heart

banana

glove

paper clip

ice-cream cone

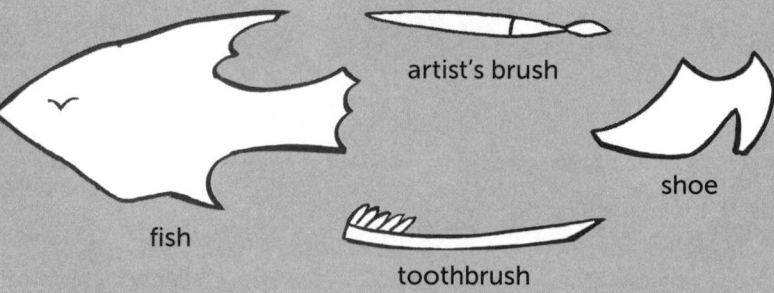
artist's brush

fish

toothbrush

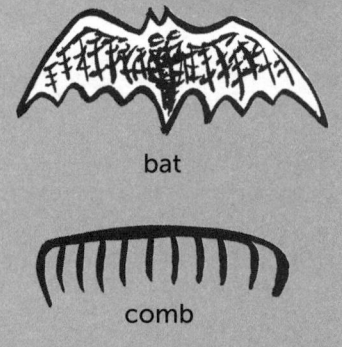
shoe

bat

comb

Art by Tim Davis

117

Forest Frolic

pennant

feather

artist's brush

cane

elf's hat

egg

snake

dolphin

heart

chick

acorn

mushroom

four-leaf clover

teacup

seashell

Art by Gary Mohrman

118

Lots to Watch

feather duster

candy cane

artist's brush

candle

ghost

glove

crescent moon

marshmallow

eyeglasses

wedge of lemon

yo-yo

arrow

snake

bacon

fish

cherry

Art by Tamara Petrosino

119

Rail Bike Trail

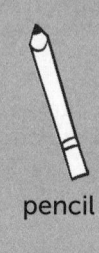
pencil

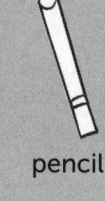
flyswatter

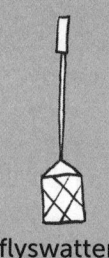
arrow

ice-cream bar

wedge of orange

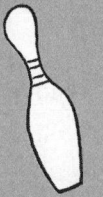
bowling pin

muffin

fish

funnel

fork

slice of cake

needle

horseshoe

mug

bat

glove

book

120

Art by Kelly Kennedy

Bird-Watchers

trowel

test tube

crescent moon

sailboat

golf tee

exclamation point

pliers

fried egg

raindrop

candy corn

drinking glass

stocking

heart

jump rope

slice of pie

ruler

hairpin

puzzle piece

chili pepper

clamshell

Art by Gary Mohrman

121

Fleas, If You Please

bowling pin

raindrop

teacup

ice-cream cone

flag

crescent moon

comb

slice of pizza

canoe

party hat

ruler

needle

sea star

bell

crayon

pencil

122

Art by Gary Mohrman

Monkey Meetup

candle

artist's brush

mug

crescent moon

sailboat

slice of watermelon

key

heart

fish

spoon

shoe

crown

airplane

Art by Maggie Swanson

123

Fishing Buddy

umbrella

carrot

banana

candle

artist's brush

lollipop

spoon

bell

toucan

soccer ball

paper airplane

mitten

balloon

shoe

tube of toothpaste

slice of cake

toothbrush

eyeglasses

Art by Chuck Dillon

My First S'more

artist's brush

mitten

balloon

party hat

carrot

golf club

toothbrush

saw

peanut

fishhook

doughnut

banana

loaf of bread

bowl

shoe

teacup

fish

Art by Marilee Harrald-Pilz

125

Zoo Crew

wishbone

award ribbon

scissors

pencil

nail

funnel

toothbrush

spoon

lightning bolt

sailboat

heart

teacup

ruler

slice of pizza

fork

126

banana

necktie

arrow

carrot

hair dryer

whale

jump rope

sock

crown

candy corn

slice of bread

potato

open book

Art by Laura Close

127

Majestic Moose

heart

cat

carrot

saw

wishbone

ice-cream cone

penguin

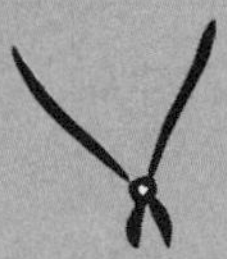

pliers

snake

lizard

needle

spoon

slice of pizza

opossum

bird

duck

Art by Tim Davis

128

Terrific Toucan

pen

kite

needle

pencil

whale

dog

bell

scissors

banana

caterpillar

fish

mouse

Art by Susan T. Hall

129

Answers

▼Pages 4–5

▼Page 6

▼Page 7

▼Page 8

▼Page 9

▼Page 10

▼Page 11

130

Answers

▼ Pages 12–13

▼ Page 14

▼ Page 15

▼ Page 16

▼ Page 17

▼ Page 18

▼ Page 19

▼ Page 20

131

Answers

▼Page 21

▼Page 22

▼Page 23

▼Pages 24–25

▼Page 26

▼Page 27

▼Page 28

▼Page 29

Answers

▼Page 30

▼Page 31

▼Page 32

▼Page 33

▼Page 34

▼Page 35

▼Pages 36–37

▼Page 38

133

Answers

▼Page 39

▼Page 40

▼Page 41

▼Page 42

▼Page 43

▼Page 44

▼Page 45

▼Pages 46–47

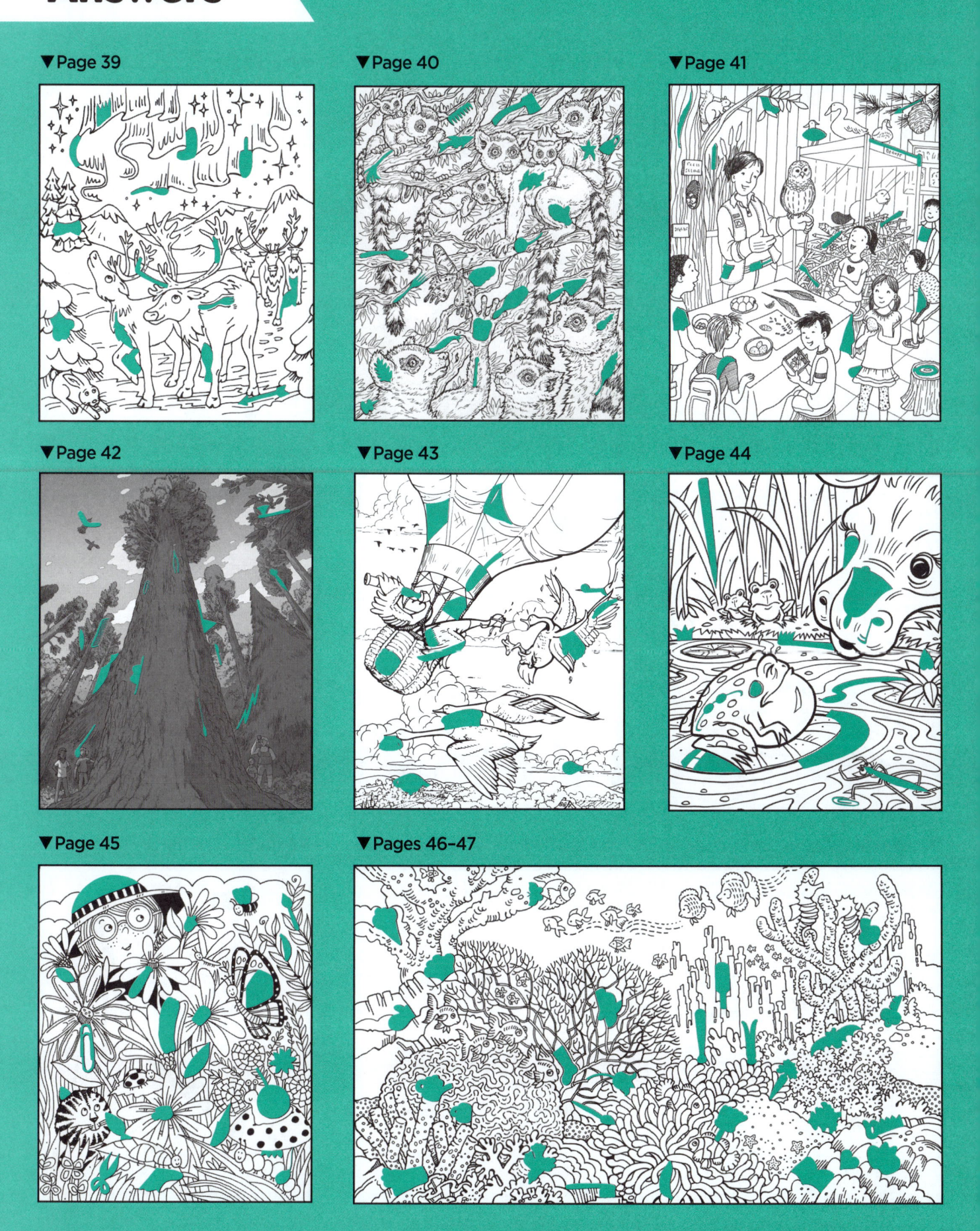

Answers

▼Page 48

▼Page 49

▼Page 50

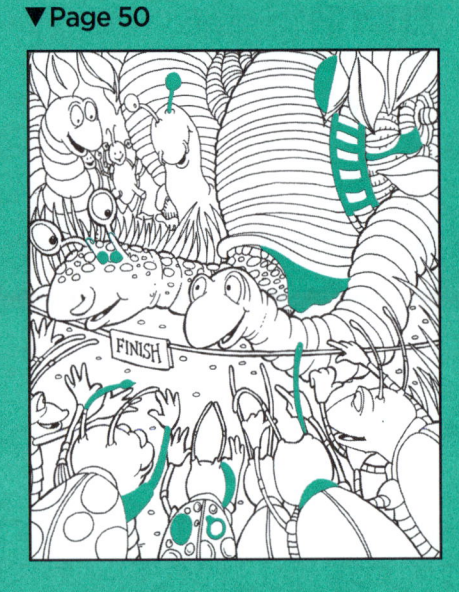

▼Page 51

▼Pages 52–53

▼Page 54

▼Page 55

▼Page 56

Answers

▼ Page 57

▼ Page 58

▼ Page 59

▼ Page 60

▼ Page 61

▼ Pages 62–63

▼ Page 64

Answers

▼ Page 65

▼ Page 66

▼ Page 67

▼ Pages 68–69

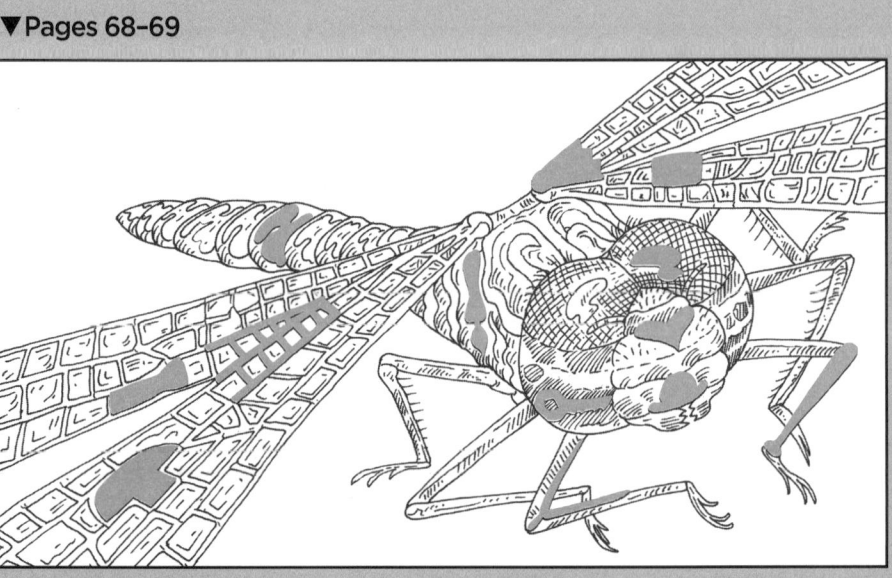

▼ Page 70

▼ Page 71

▼ Page 72

▼ Page 73

137

Answers

▼Page 74

▼Page 75

▼Pages 76–77

▼Page 78

▼Page 79

▼Page 80

138

Answers

▼Page 81

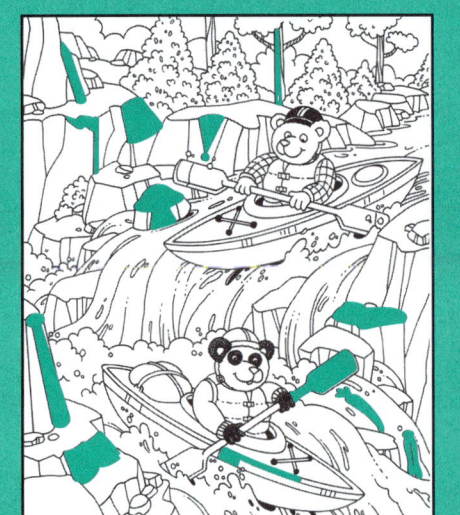

▼Page 82

▼Page 83

▼Page 84

▼Page 85

▼Pages 86–87

▼Page 88

139

Answers

▼Page 89

▼Page 90

▼Page 91

▼Page 92

▼Page 93

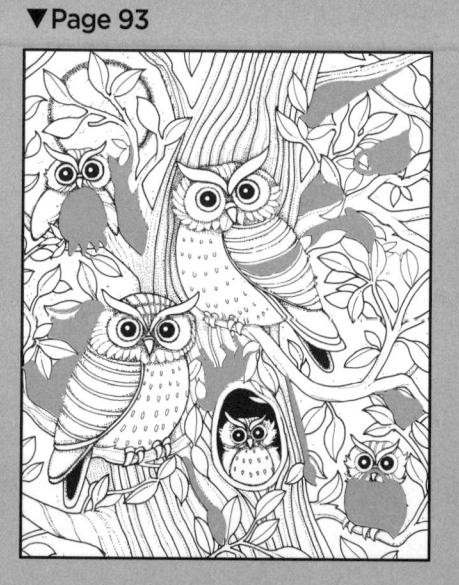

▼Pages 94–95

▼Page 96

140

Answers

▼Page 97

▼Page 98

▼Page 99

▼Pages 100–101

▼Page 102

▼Page 103

▼Page 104

▼Page 105

141

Answers

▼ Page 106

▼ Page 107

▼ Pages 108–109

▼ Page 110

▼ Page 111

▼ Page 112

▼ Page 113

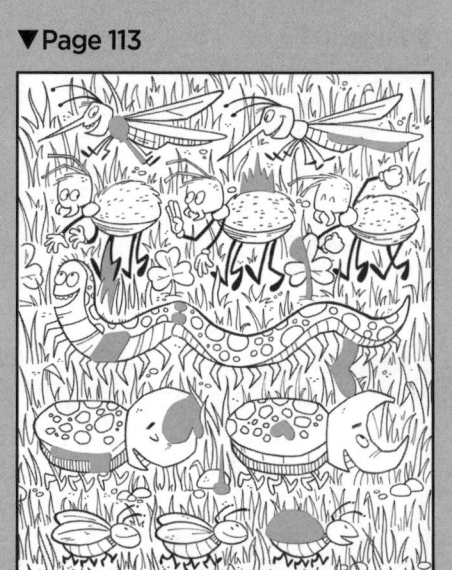

142

Answers

▶ Pages 114–115

▶ Page 116

▶ Page 117

▶ Page 118

▶ Page 119

▶ Page 120

▶ Page 121

▶ Page 122

143

Answers

▲ Page 129

▲ Pages 126–127

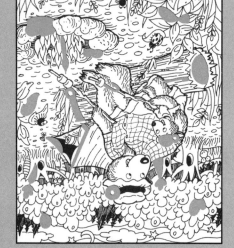
▲ Page 128

▲ Page 125

▲ Page 124

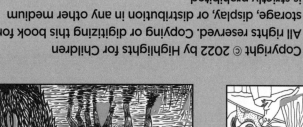
▲ Page 123

Copyright © 2022 by Highlights for Children
All rights reserved. Copying or digitizing this book for storage, display, or distribution in any other medium is strictly prohibited.

For information about permission to reprint selections from this book, please contact permissions@highlights.com.

Published by Highlights Press
815 Church Street, Honesdale, Pennsylvania 18431
ISBN: 978-1-64472-868-0
Manufactured in Dongguan, Guangdong, China
Mfg. 08/2024
First edition
Visit our website at Highlights.com.

10 9 8 7 6 5 4 3

144